Follow the Star

Christmas Songs for Piano
Level 2

Donna Gielow McFarland, editor and arranger
Cherry Wilson and Tami Wilson, arrangers
Illustrated by Sandy Silverthorne

Also by Donna McFarland

Music Instruction

Follow the Star: Christmas Songs for Piano (Primer - Level 5)
Worship at the Keys: A Method Book
Intro to Piano: Class Piano for Adult Beginners
Music Theory Made Simpl(er)
Intervals, Scales and Chords (oh, my!)

Stories for Kids

Duck and Friends Early Readers

Duck and Friends: The Dinosaur Bones
Duck and Friends: The Computer Chase

The Purple Elephant Chapter Books

The Purple Elephant
The Purple Elephant: The Journey Home

Sam and the Dragon: A Medieval Mars Story

Also included in *Medieval Mars: The Anthology*

Contributed Piano Compositions and Arrangements to:

Hymns 'n Spirituals at Your Fingertips
Folk Songs 'n Favorites at Your Fingertips
Fast Track Solos

Published by Spencer Meadow Press

Printed in the U.S.A.
First Edition, May 2019

Table of Contents

The Holly and the Ivy

French Carol
Arranged by Donna McFarland

Both hands play one octave up on repeat

Moderato

The hol-ly and the i-vy, When they are both full grown, Of __

all the trees that are in the wood, The __ hol-ly bears the crown.

1

We Three Kings

John H. Hopkins
Arranged by Donna McFarland

Stately

We three kings of O - ri - ent are,

Bear - ing gifts we trav - erse a - far,

Field and foun - tain, moor and moun ___ tain,

Fol - low - ing yon - der star. O ___

Star of won - der, star of night,

Star with roy - al beau - ty bright;

West - ward lead - ing, still pro - ceed - ing,

Guide us to thy per - fect light.

3

Silent Night

Franz Gruber
Arranged by Tami Wilson

Hold damper pedal down throughout.

Si _____ lent   night,   ho _____ ly   night!

4

All is calm, all is bright.

Round yon Vir____gin Moth - er and Child,

Ho - ly In - fant so ten - der and mild,

Sleep in heav - en - ly peace,____

Sleep___ in heav - en - ly peace.___

loco

pp

LH 5 RH 1

rit.

LH

The First Noel

English Carol
Arranged by Donna McFarland

Moderato

mf The __ first _____ No __ el the __ an - gel did
fields _____ where they lay __ keep - ing their

say, Was to cer - tain poor shep - herds in fields as they
sheep On a cold win - ter's night ____ that was ____ so

lay; In __ No __ el, _____ No __ el. No __ el, No -
deep.

el. Born is the King __ of Is ____ ra __ el.

O Come, O Come Emmanuel

Thomas Helmore
Arranged by Donna McFarland

Solemnly

mp O come, O come, Em - man — u - el, _____ And

ran - som cap - tive Is _____ ra - el, _____ That

mourns in lone - ly ex _____ ile here, _____ Un -

til the Son of God ___ ap - pear. ___ **f** Re -

joice! Re - joice! Em - man ___ u -

el shall come to thee, O Is ___ ra -

el! ___ *mp* Re ___

We Wish You a Merry Christmas

English Folk Song
Arranged by Cherry Wilson

Like a fanfare

wish you a Mer-ry Christ-mas. We wish you a Mer-ry Christ-mas. We

wish you a Mer-ry Christ-mas and a Hap - py New Year! Yeah! We

f

1.

2.

Year! *mp*

mf

f

ff

What Child is This? (duet)

English Carol
Arranged by Donna McFarland

Play part I one octave higher than written

Lyrics: What child is this, who, laid to rest on Ma - ry's lap __ is sleep - ing? Whom an - gels greet __ with an - thems

Lyrics:
sweet_ While shep herds watch_ are keep - ing? This, this __ is

Christ the King, Whom shep - herds guard and an - gels sing:

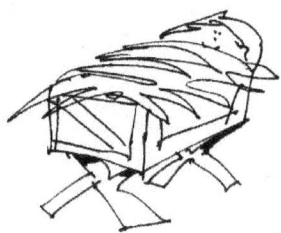

Haste, haste to bring Him laud, the Babe, the son of Ma - ry.

rit.

I Wonder as I Wander

Appalachian Carol adapted by John Jacob Niles
Arranged by Donna McFarland

Thoughtfully

mp I won - der as I wan - der out un - der the sky, How

with pedal

Je - sus, the Sav - ior, did come for to die. For

poor, or - nery peo - ple like you and like I. I

won - der as I wan - der, Out un - der the sky.

Theme from
Nutcracker Suite Overture

Tchaikovsky
Arranged by Donna McFarland

Auld Lang Syne

Robert Burns

Arranged by Donna McFarland

Wistfully

Should auld ac-quaint-ance be for-got, and nev - er brought to mind? Should auld ac-quaint - ance be for-got and___ days of Auld Lang Syne.

rit.

About the Arrangers

Donna Gielow McFarland received a B.Mus. in Piano Performance from Wheaton College and an M.Mus. in Piano Pedagogy from the University of Oregon. She has taught music classes at Northwest Christian University, New Hope Christian College (formerly Eugene Bible College) and the University of Oregon. Donna published several original piano compositions and arrangements with The Lorenz Company. She also writes stories for children and textbooks for music theory and class piano.
Visit Donna at: duckandfriends.com

Cherry Wilson has had many musical adventures in her life including teaching (preschool through college), accompanying, performing and arranging. She earned a B.A. in Music from Columbia Christian College, an M.Mus. in Piano Pedagogy and an M.A. in Music History, both from the University of Oregon.

Tami Wilson loves operating her own piano studio, Music with Tami, where she teaches students to create music on the piano. She also loves being part of the worship band at her church. Tami has a B.A. in Humanities, with an emphasis in music, from Thomas Edison State College.
Visit Tami at: musicwithtami.wordpress.com

About the Illustrator

Sandy Silverthorne is an award-winning author/illustrator with over half a million copies in print. His Great Bible Adventure children's series has been distributed in eight languages worldwide. Sandy has worked as a cartoonist, author, illustrator, actor, pastor, speaker, and comedian. Apparently it's hard for him to focus.
Connect with Sandy at sandysilverthornebooks.com

Follow the Star Collection

Primer & Level 1

A set of arrangements of 14 well-known Christmas songs including Jingle Bells, Silent Night, We Three Kings and Up on the Housetop. Primer arrangements are as easy as possible with only one note at a time. Some songs have optional teacher accompaniments. The Level 1 arrangements contain some hands-together playing. Perfect for piano students who just started lessons in the fall and want to play music for Christmas.

Level 2

These simple yet beautiful arrangements of well-known Christmas songs span the distance from easy Level 2 to almost ready for Level 3. Left hand parts include single notes, intervals and primary triads. * We Three Kings * Silent Night * We Wish You a Merry Christmas * O Come, O Come Emmanuel * What Child is This? (duet) * The First Noel * I Wonder as I Wander * Auld Lang Syne * The Holly and the Ivy * Nutcracker Suite Overture Theme *

Level 3

This lively Level 3 collection of Christmas songs includes a bouncy Jingle Bells, Carol of the Bells simple enough to play at a quick tempo, a fresh arrangement of Go, Tell it On the Mountain, the jazzy Horses and Bells, the full 12 Days of Christmas, and a dreamy What Child is This? Also included are traditional Hark! The Herald Angels Sing, O Little Town of Bethlehem, and the Nutcracker Suite's Dance of the Sugar Plum Fairy and Waltz of the Flowers.

Level 4

A collection of fresh new arrangements of 10 Christmas songs. These arrangements can be used as a pedagogical tool along with students' regular lesson repertoire. Level 4 includes a slow, dreamy Silent Night, Deck the Halls with a staccato ostinato bass line, a bouncy version of Away in the Manger (for Cowboys), and a traditional sing-a-long Joy to the World. Also included are: March of the Toy Soldiers (from the Nutcracker Suite), Good Christian Men, Rejoice!, Lo! How a Rose E're Blooming, Angels We Have Heard on High, A Thousand Candles and Good King Wenceslas.

Level 5

A collection of Christmas arrangements for the intermediate piano student, designed to be both functional and pleasing. Selections include the beautiful Mary, Did You Know?, a traditional O Holy Night, Pachelbel's Canon with a Christmas twist, Russian Dance (from the Nutcracker Suite), a sing-a-long carol medley, an original carol by composer Gene Skinner and a lively First Five Days of Christmas, which is based on the traditional 12 Days of Christmas. This fresh new version ends with a boogie-woogie on Day 5 as the gift recipient pleads for no more birds.

Fake Book

This entry-level fake book features 24 well-known Christmas songs in lead sheet notation – melody, lyrics and chord symbols. A step-by-step tutorial shows players new to improvisation a method for getting started. All songs are in singable keys with no more than two sharps or flats in the key signature. Chords are simplified and melodies are in large, easy-to-read music notation. * Jingle Bells * Silent Night * Joy to the World * We Three Kings * O Holy Night * What Child is This? * The First Noel * We Wish You a Merry Christmas* and many more.

www.ingramcontent.com/pod-product-compliance
Lightning Source LLC
Chambersburg PA
CBHW081236020426
42331CB00012B/3206